MW01291459

How to Take Your Clothes Off

A Guide to Nudism
for the Interested Beginner

By Matthew McDermott

Follow the author on Twitter: **@canudian1**

Check out the author's web page:
writenude.com

Join the nudist community on reddit at
www.reddit.com/r/nudism

Contents

Introduction

Who this Book Is For

Maybe no one knows it yet—and maybe you're not sure yourself—but you're a nudist.

You feel good when you're not wearing anything.

It's not a sexual thing. It's a physical thing: you're more comfortable without clothes on. And maybe it's an emotional or spiritual thing too: you feel better, more at peace when you're not wearing anything.

Our society isn't friendly to this idea. Nudity is inextricably linked to sexuality in the modern world, so someone who is nude when others aren't is considered a freak or an aberration. They're not, but that's how society usually regards them.

People don't feel comfortable with the suggestion of nudity, either. People snigger at anyone who is not clothed in the most conventional way. They slut-shame women who dare to be topless in parks, even if it is perfectly legal (and those women are often harassed by the police as well). People get angry, they turn into giggling children, they point and laugh.

In popular media, nudity is highly sexually charged. Bare flesh is displayed suggestively on the bodies of perfectly-toned young men and women. It's almost never depicted as something positive or even unremarkable. If skin is shown, it's the skin of an extremely good-looking person, according to the prevailing standards of beauty.

When regular people are depicted nude in the media, they are presented as something ridiculous or even offensive. And when actual nudists are described, it's usually in openly mocking and insulting terms. Most news stories involving nudists are full of tiresome puns using childish language for nudity and the body, like "bare facts" and "butt out". They also use outdated terms like "nudist colony" which perpetuate negative stereotypes.

Despite all of that, despite the negative messages you've received all your life about modesty, despite the sexualization that is intensely applied to the subject, you've recognized the truth.

You like to be nude.

If this is where you ended up, and you're wondering what to do about that, then this book is for you.

About Me

A few years ago, I really needed this book.

When I was young, I found myself with my clothes off a lot. I slept naked whenever I felt I could get away with it, pyjamas tucked beside me in case I had to run out of the room for some emergency. I remember swimming around in a lake with my bathing suit clutched firmly in my hand, enjoying the feeling of water all around me. In grade eight, I played sick multiple times to be able to spend a day at home, alone, naked.

I was raised as a Roman Catholic by parents who were very uncomfortable about nudity. Because of their values, I was afraid of my preference for nudity and what it said about me as a person. Was I a deviant? And so, as I entered my confusing puberty years, I worked hard to ignore my nudist tendencies.

It wasn't until my early thirties that I discovered online nudist groups. I was stunned to find that there were others who shared the preference for having no clothes on. They weren't perverts. They weren't sexual deviants. They weren't freaks. They just liked to be nude.

After I realized that there was a whole community of nudists, I went to a nude beach for the first time. It was a wonderful experience. Then I went to a nudist resort. It was even better.

Now I'm a regular nudist, and I am active in the nudist community. I know very well the worries, questions, and fears that people have as they enter the nudist world.

I also know that overcoming those fears is worth it.

If you feel the pull, but haven't found a way to overcome your doubts and fears, you need someone to give you information, perspective, and encouragement. You need practical advice, without judgement, that will help you discover the positive difference that nudism can make in your life.

You have nothing to lose but your hang-ups, shame, and baggage.

And, of course, your clothes.

What Is Nudism?

Nudism is a simple concept: it's the preference, in a normally clothed society, for not wearing clothes.

There are many simple reasons to be nude: to a lot of people, it simply feels better. It feels better outside, especially, where your whole body can feel the air and the wind and the sun.

Many people also find that being nude has positive emotional, psychological, and spiritual effects. The effect of freeing yourself from artificial coverings makes your mind freer, too. Nudists tend to be at a place of acceptance with their own bodies, as well as with others'. The idea that bodies are something to be judged or criticized—especially by one's own self—tends to fall away when we stop relying on clothing to define ourselves.

Most societies also make a strong association between nudity and sexuality. Because many people are never nude with others except in a sexual situation, many people assume that nudity itself is intrinsically sexual. While it's true that one is often nude while having sex, the association doesn't necessarily go the other way. There's nothing inherently sexual about nudity, and if you ask any medical professional, art model, or person in the shower, they would agree.

So what's so different about nudism? It is this: nudists prefer to be nude, even in situations where nudity is not normally found. Nudists might cook, watch TV, and mop their kitchen floor while they're nude. They often sleep nude. They might hike, swim, and hang out with other people while all of them are nude. They might go bowling, socialize in a pub, and play sports nude.

Nudists recognize the increase in happiness and health that they gain from being nude. Whether on their own or with other people, they are nude more often than others, and in situations where people might not normally be nude.

That's all there is to nudism. It's very simple, but practicing as a nudist with other people in a nudity-averse society can be difficult.

And that's what the rest of this book is for.

Some Myths

Given the way society views nudity, it is unsurprising that many myths have developed about nudism. Most people are uncomfortable or embarrassed even thinking about being nude, which means they accept these myths without questioning. Here are some of the biggest myths about nudity, and a few words about the reality that nudists know and experience.

Myth 1: All Nudists Are Beautiful

When nude beaches or resorts are depicted in movies—whether they actually show nude people or cover them up—most of the nudists in the scenes are young, athletic, and beautiful. This image of lean beautiful women and thin, muscular young men is so persistent that many think that they couldn't possibly expose their old, fat, or otherwise imperfect body among these wonderful, beautiful things.

It's absolutely false. There are nudists who are attractive by modern society's beauty standards and there are others who are not. Look around at the mix of people on your subway train or in your mall. That's exactly what you'll find in a nudist venue. What you'll see is humanity, in all its many versions of perfection. Nudists don't have a certain body type, and there is no standard to which they have to conform.

Myth 2: All Nudists Are Ugly/Old/Fat

The opposite myth is also prevalent. Nudists are often the object of ridicule in the media, so the easy joke is that nudists are people who don't look like the nude or nearly-nude models that are commonly shown in the media. It is a popular rejection of nudist culture for some people, too: numerous times, I've heard the comment "the only people who are at nudist places are people you wouldn't want to see nude".

First, nudists know that you don't go to nudist places to see nude people, or to be seen by others. Social nudity is about *being*, first and foremost. We'll talk about this more later in this book.

The statement also says a lot about the speaker's own unhealthy misconceptions about nudity and nudism, and it's also completely false. At almost any nudist venue, there is a mix of body types and ages. I've seen nudists too elderly to walk without a walker or cane; I've seen children of all ages happily splashing in the pool. I've seen extremely obese people and extremely skinny people. I've seen people who could be Olympic athletes or supermodels. I've seen the full spectrum of human bodies during the time I've spent in nudist spaces. There is no "typical" nudist body, any more than there is a typical human body.

Myth 3: Nudists Are Nude All the Time

Some non-nudists take the idea of nudism to be an all-encompassing thing. They figure that if someone is a nudist, they must be nude every moment of the day. (There was an episode of Family Guy with a nudist family that was depicted like this. It was an unfortunate, intolerant, and unfunny view of nudism.)

Of course, this is a myth. There is no required amount of nudity in order to be a nudist, and nudism can be practiced in a number of different ways. (See **Types of Naturism** for more on this.) Nudism is a *preference for being unclothed*. It isn't a compulsion, and it isn't something that most nudists do in defiance of social norms.

Nudists also aren't stupid. If they're cold, they cover up. If they are in non-nudist spaces, they cover up. In general, nudists are nude only when it's appropriate. Of course, they look more regularly for appropriate places to be nude than the average person, too. But almost no one has the opportunity to be nude all the time. Our society just doesn't work that way.

Myth 4: Nudists Want to Expose Themselves to Others

With nudity being a source of fear and shame for others, some people may project those negative feelings onto others. They might assume that anyone who chooses to be nude is doing so for attention, or for a sexual thrill, or to make others uncomfortable. When they think that negative emotions must be associated with nudity, they try to rationalize the preference for nudity according to those negative ideas.

When it comes down to it, nudists are typically nude only for themselves. Yes, it's nice to be around other people who understand that preference for nudity. Yes, it's lovely to experience friendships that look past those artificial barriers and fake personas that we build up in regular society. But in the end, a nudist is a nudist because they like to be nude. Exposing themselves to other people is not even a consideration when it comes to getting naked.

Myth 5: Nudity Is Harmful

Part of the fear and shame around nudism leads people to believe that there is some harm in being nude. They suspect that a nudist is trying to use nudity against other people, in the way an exhibitionist would. And because child pornography is a serious issue in our society, people are taught to be on guard for the sight of nude children.

Nudists are no different from anyone else in condemning the sexualization of children. However, if the human body itself is neither harmful nor shameful, there is no reason to associate mere nudity with sex, even with children. That means that there is nothing wrong with children being present and being nude in safe nudist environments. In fact, there is some evidence that nudism is positive for children, leading them to grow up with a healthier self-image and a more accepting, body-positive attitude towards themselves and others.

There is one caveat, however, especially involving children. Some unscrupulous businesses make money by recording videos of family nudist events—parties, visits to swimming pools, saunas, and more—to appeal to consumers who are turned on by seeing nude children. In some cases, groups of teenagers are hired to be nude on camera, pretending to partake in some activities together. These videos are exploitative and wrong, and do not represent nudism in any way. Family nudism is far different from videos of nude children.

Myth 6: Nudity Is Sinful

One of the oldest stories in western civilization is the Old Testament story of the Garden of Eden. After discovering sin, Adam and Eve cover up, as the sight of their unclothed bodies seem, for the first time, shameful. Religions often emphasize modesty, shame people for being nude, and suppress ideas of body freedom. Whatever their purpose— whether it's meant to help people or not—it leads many people who grew up in religious households to consider nudity to be a shameful, sinful thing.

While many religious groups do have various rules or issues around nudity, nudists include practitioners from many different religious faiths as well. There are Christian nudists, Muslim nudists, Mormon nudists, and Hindu nudists, and a number of online forums and groups for nudists of other religious traditions. It is up to the individual to resolve their faith with the practice of naturism. But rest assured that others have come to the conclusion that nudism is not necessarily in conflict with their beliefs.

Of course, I respect any person's religious beliefs, and would not counsel anyone to go against their own conscience. But from the number of people I have come across who are able to reconcile nudism with their religious beliefs, I suspect that it is indeed possible to make the two compatible.

Myth 7: Nudism Is Sexual

As we discussed earlier, nudity is closely associated with sexuality in modern western society. In fact, for many people, nudity is only experienced when washing, changing clothes, or having sex. A relaxed, accepting attitude towards nudity may be something they have never experienced at any point in their lives. Thus when they hear about groups of people who get together nude, or even large properties where people gather and are completely nude together, their imaginations run wild. Nudists, they decide, are sex-crazed people who have massive orgies.

In fact, the opposite is true. In a nudist environment, the actual nudity—the "naughty bits" that are so often hidden from view—soon becomes commonplace and even boring. It's really an interesting effect, one that many new nudists are surprised to experience for the first time. When we are nude and around other nude people, our minds tend to completely desexualize the situation. Many first-time nudists are pleasantly surprised at how comfortable the environment is, and how free it is of sexual tensions.

What's more, most nudists are quite sensitive to this myth and discourage sexual acts in public in nudist places. It's grounds for being removed or even banned from most nudist resorts. That's not to say that nudists aren't ever sexual with each other; they just keep that side of things private, as most people do.

Why Be Nude?

You wouldn't be reading this book if you weren't at least curious about the nudist experience. But many people who are new to nudism are unaware of all the reasons they might want to be nude.

One of the reasons many people prefer nudity is the most simple physical reason: it's more comfortable. Many people who are not nudists know the pure joy of unhooking a bra or kicking off socks at the end of a long day. Losing the constrictive bindings that grasp our bodies most of the time can be a joyful moment, even more so when you can get all your clothes off and let your body breathe.

That comfort is even greater when doing some activities. If you've never been swimming nude, you're in for one of the most wonderful physical sensations you'll ever feel.

But these are physical sensations. There are less tangible and more important reasons for taking your clothes off too. Nudism isn't just a mode of physical comfort. You will find that the state of mind can be a major benefit of being nude.

Even when you're completely alone, being nude enables you to relate to your body in a more real, meaningful way. Clothes are a barrier to sensations. When you're nude, you awaken the sense of touch across your whole body. The movement of air, the feeling of temperature—and if you're outside, the sensation of sunlight—are no longer processed through a wall of textiles or on a limited patch of skin or hair.

There are plenty of reasons to be nude, and very few reasons not to be nude. If you can put aside the ideas of shame that our society has perpetuated for your entire life, you can be nude and embrace your truest self.

Getting Started

Almost everyone starts out as a nudist in the same place: at home. It's much easier to "try on" nudity with some privacy and familiar surroundings. (If you don't need to practice being nude at home, great! Move on to other nudist opportunities, if you want.)

Most likely, you're nude at home more than anywhere else. Taking showers or baths and changing clothes are the most common reasons to be nude. And this is the best place to start.

Practicing Nudism at Home

The safety and comfort of your own home is the best place to practice nudity for the first time.

If you live alone, it's really easy: just take your clothes off. It will probably feel weird at first: you're used to having clothes on so having nothing on is a strange sensation. But that's where to start.

If you don't live alone, and you're worried about how your roommates or family will react, then the easiest place to start is in your own bed. Try sleeping nude for a night.

If you share your bed, then your partner might react in some way. Because nudity is so often associated with sex, it might seem like an invitation to your partner. (And there's nothing wrong with that if you're willing, of course!) But by the second or third night, it will feel more normal, both to you and to your partner.

Often, new nudists fear what their partner will think if they start sleeping nude all the time. What if your spouse asks, "why are you sleeping naked so much these days?" It might seem like a difficult question to answer, but the best response is the truth. Why *do* you prefer to be naked? It's more comfortable. It feels better. It helps you sleep better. Whatever your answer, just say it. And when you do, you've taken a step forward in normalizing nudism in your home.

Another common concern is that your children will see you naked. As you can imagine, nudist families see each other nude all the time, but if you're the first nudist in your household it might be a shocking notion. However, unless your children crawl into bed with you, they're unlikely to ever know you're nude under the covers. If your children do get into bed, even from time to time (nightmares are scary!), it's worth thinking about how to handle it.

If your children are very young, they probably won't take much notice of your state of dress. If they do ask, "Why is daddy naked?" the simple, honest answer is still best. Maybe it will open up a conversation about nudity and bodies that will be helpful to your children even if they never practice nudism themselves. In any case, you'll want to discuss this with your partner before it happens—and your partner may bring up the issue anyway.

Remember also that we often wear less clothing in bed. A nightie, a pair of boxers, no socks, no bra—it isn't that much of a leap to be nude. Being naked is only a step further, and it's typically only in our minds that it's such a big step.

However, especially where children are involved, your partner may object to your being nude in bed. Sometimes you have to pick your battles; nighttime naturism just might not be something your family is ready for yet.

Other Opportunities

Part of becoming an active naturist is finding opportunities when you can be nude. Working around a spouse or family isn't always easy, but the more you are naked, the more comfortable and relaxed you'll be. (I can personally attest that if I have more nude time, I feel better clothed as well.)

The easiest opportunity for many is to get undressed when you're home alone. If you've got an afternoon, an hour, or even twenty minutes of solitude, get undressed. Don't make a big deal of it; do whatever you would do at the same time clothed. You can cook, read your twitter feed, watch baseball, or write your novel nude. That's the point: it's not "special" to be nude. (You might feel safer if you have some clothing—shorts and a t-shirt, for example—near at hand, in case you don't have quite as much alone time as you expected.)

If you have a private space—say, your own room if you live with roommates or family, or the master bedroom if you have a spouse—then this can also be a nude space. Most people, even parents and partners, understand that everyone needs some privacy from time to time. Whatever space you have where you can be alone, you can use it to be nude.

What if someone comes crashing into your private space while you're nude? Remember— it's embarrassing for everyone. And *they* are interrupting *you*. Most likely, they'll apologize and back out. (They'll probably laugh, too: this is their response to their surprise and nervousness, and likely not directed at you.) At that time or later, they might ask why you were nude. Again, the honest answer is the simplest and best answer: you felt like it, and you were alone in your room.

Sometimes it's difficult to choose a moment to say "I'll get undressed now." You might try adding a bit of time when you're already undressed to simply enjoy being nude. After you come out of the shower or bath, when you're changing out of your work or school clothes, when you get up in the morning. You don't have to do anything special. You're in your most natural state; just act natural. After a while, you may find it easier to get past the hesitation, and you won't need an "excuse" to be naked.

If you're having trouble finding a safe space to be nude, here's another idea: wear a robe with nothing on under it. Even when the robe is closed and the belt is securely knotted, it's not quite the same feeling as having clothes on your body. A robe with nothing underneath can be a safe way to get close of the sensation of being nude. You can close it quickly if someone comes along, and your roommates and family will likely think you have pyjamas or underwear on underneath.

Nudity and Respect

An important aspect of trying out nudism with other people around is respect—for yourself and for others. There is nothing wrong with your desire to be nude. It's a perfectly natural state. However, there's nothing wrong with others not wanting to see you nude, either.

Some nudists try to push the envelope and impose their nudity on others without their consent. They feel that because they are comfortable with nudity, others ought to be just as comfortable, so they'll take their clothes off in inappropriate situations or expose themselves to others without their consent.

This can also be true for nudists interacting with non-nudists. A local swim group I've attended had to tell male participants not to talk to the female lifeguards at the nude swims and try to convince them to try nudism, for example. This kind of behaviour is aggressive and disrespectful. When people are doing their job or going about their daily business, they should not feel like someone is forcing them into a situation that is uncomfortable for them.

As nudists, we know how good it feels to release ourselves from the burdens of clothing, and it's hard not to want others to experience the same rush of life-affirming freedom. However, just as nudists wish to have the choice to remove their clothes without stigma or shame, we must respect non-nudists' choice to remain clothed. And when we practice nudism, we must ensure that those who will see and interact with us will not be shocked or upset by our nudity. In a body-hiding, nudity-shaming society, this is sadly an important consideration, even in our own homes.

Naturism is about respect in many dimensions: respect for ourselves and our bodies, respect for others' bodies, and respect for the world around us. Our enthusiasm for naturism must fit in with the realities of our society, though, and that means respecting those who are not naturists as well.

Common Questions

Almost anyone trying nudism for the first time will have a number of questions and doubts as they think about actually getting nude with other people, so let's get some of the scary questions out of the way. These questions often make the very idea of nudism seem too daunting to try, but usually the answers are easier than the nascent nudist expects.

We'll look at questions that almost everyone asks, followed by questions that are gender-specific.

Questions from Everyone

If you're new to nudism and social nudity, you undoubtedly have some questions. Rest assured that your questions are probably ones that others have asked before. And there's no judgement here: your concerns and your fears are real and legitimate. But by reading through these questions and answers, I hope you'll find some confidence for your first nudist outing.

What is the difference between the terms "nudist" and "naturist"?

Some people feel that these terms are interchangeable. Others argue that one or the other is preferable for them. It's important to recognize that neither term has an "official" definition, and that they are almost always used interchangeably.

The term "nudist" is perhaps the more widely-used term. It is accurate and descriptive: we are people who prefer to be nude. It doesn't confine someone to a certain lifestyle: they could be nude only within their own home, or only once a year at a resort. They could still be a nudist.

It also differentiates them from people who are naked on occasion, in certain situations. Someone who goes skinny-dipping with friends every once in a while might be nude socially only in that specific situation. That person may not want to identify as a nudist. (And that's fine of course!)

However, some in the clothes-free community reject the term nudist. They worry about the associations and assumptions that society makes about nudists—associations that are misguided and wrong, but persist anyway. For many, the word "nudist" almost automatically suggests the next word as "colony", which is an outdated term.

Some also have a philosophical objection to the term. They don't define themselves merely as someone who likes to have their clothes off. Their nudity is part of a wider worldview that is about being closer to nature, others, and themselves. (We'll talk more about this worldview, called "ethical naturism", later in this book.)

The most common alternative term to nudist is "naturist". This is a little less direct, but it reflects a person's desire to be in a more natural state. People who reject the term "nudist" on philosophical grounds tend to gravitate towards "naturist" because it connects to their worldview that we cannot truly be ourselves if we hide behind clothing.

While few people seem to dislike the term naturist, it does have its own problems. The most common one is that it is commonly confused with the term "naturalist", which is used to describe nature enthusiasts. It is not necessarily a good thing to have people show up to a nudist event expecting a hike in the woods looking at birds and wildflowers, so don't confuse the terms. (Of course you can be both a naturist and a naturalist, but there might not be a lot of overlap between the groups.)

In the end, though, the two terms are very similar. They do not necessarily denote any particular philosophy or mindset, other than a preference to be naked. In this book, the terms are considered interchangeable.

Will my body look out of place? Aren't I too fat, skinny, small, large, wrong in some dimension?

I've heard it so often from new naturists. "I'd like to go but I really should lose ten pounds first." "My parts are too big, too small, too strange." "I don't want to be seen like this!"

It's hard to believe, but because we're all sharing in the same open and trusting environment, nudists really and sincerely don't care about what each other's bodies look like. I've met extremely fat nudists and almost anorexic-looking nudists. Parts of the anatomy of every size and shape. Older nudists using walkers and canes. One of the most amazing things about the nudist experience is that you get to see how flawed—and how beautiful—every human body is.

Of course, society's beauty standards still exist. Fit, shapely, and generally good-looking people often look good out of their clothes, too. But in a nude environment, it's uncanny how little any of that matters. We're all just who we are when we're in our own skin. I've never seen or heard anyone in a nudist environment being shamed or embarrassed for their body size or shape. It's exactly the opposite of the nudist philosophy.

What about my scars, birthmarks, and other anomalies?

People who have marks on their body—scars from injuries or surgeries, birth abnormalities, or other conditions—are often self-conscious of them. It's important to know that no matter what it's been through, your body is welcome in a nudist space.

I've seen women who had been through partial, single, and double mastectomies. I've seen people with missing limbs, extensive and noticeable birthmarks, and protuberances from various parts of their bodies. And again, they've been as comfortable as anyone else.

The point of nudism is not to show off bodily perfection, and it is not to provide a view of other nude people. It's not about seeing or being seen. It's about being. No matter what your body looks like, what character your skin shows. Your body is welcome.

What if I run into someone I know while I'm nude?

If you're interested in nudism, you have probably already felt less of the shame and embarrassment that many of us have learned to associate with nudity. However, it is still common to feel vulnerable when nude, and the idea of running into someone you know in your regular life while you're nude can make you feel even more vulnerable.

This is why it's so common to fear encountering someone you know—family member, coworker, or even distant acquaintance—while you're nude. You think you'll be exposed and in a real position of weakness. And of course that person will tell everyone you know about your preference.

There are a couple of reasons why you don't need to worry about this. First, if you're at a nudist venue, they will probably be just as nude as you are. This is one of the most marvellous things about being a nudist: everyone is on equal footing. Traditional power imbalances dissolve into a sense of community and shared trust.

It's also unlikely that anyone you run into at a nudist venue will share your secret with anyone else. If they're a nudist they will be familiar with how important discretion can be while talking about the subject. And to "out" you, they would have to explain how they came to meet you at a nudist venue... which they were obviously at themselves.

In fact, running into someone you know is probably worth looking forward to. They are now someone with whom you have something in common, other than nudism itself. You might have a moment of awkwardness with them as you both adjust your images of each other. But your fears are generally completely unfounded.

What if someone finds out I'm a nudist?

This is another very common fear—and it typically seems much bigger than it actually is. The most dramatic responses are usually rolled eyes, an embarrassed giggle, or "Neat!" Nudity is a taboo subject, especially in North America, and some find it embarrassing to even discuss the subject. They might also have misconceptions about nudists and could project these misconceptions onto you.

Most of the time, though, your friends and family will not react as strongly as you probably expect. That only makes sense: most people really don't care what you wear around the house, or when they're not around.

Some people who are more uncomfortable about the idea might worry that you're going to force your openness on them. This is probably because nudists are often depicted this way in movies and on TV: as people who have no idea that everyone else isn't a nudist, and who constantly and casually expose themselves, with or without others' consent. Perhaps there are one or two nudists out there like this, but the vast majority are not. Unfortunately, our media pushes this myth so much that many people believe it is true.

Again, the shame and embarrassment that our society attaches to nudity makes this fear seem much larger than it actually is. Even if you get a smirk or a giggle from someone who discovers you're a nudist, it is usually quickly forgotten by that person. Think about what the real consequences would be if some friends found out you went to a nude beach. You might be mildly embarrassed, but it's not the end of the world. And you might find out that some of your friends are more open-minded than you thought.

There are exceptions of course. Some people worry that they could lose their job if their employer discovered they were a nudist. Others have a justifiable fear of being shunned or ostracized from their social group, for example if they belong to a very conservative family or community organization. In these cases, discretion is much more important. Most nudist resorts understand this, however. They are typically careful to protect the identities of their guests, and won't send mail or e-mail unless you specifically give them permission to.

For any nudist organization or business, it is absolutely fine to inquire what their privacy policy is before you attend them. If it isn't sufficient for your needs, or if they don't have one, then stay away.

Questions from Men

Can I go to a nudist venue as a single man?

There are a number of nudist resorts, particularly in the USA, where single men are not allowed to attend. There are also some nudist events that only allow single women and couples.

The reason, of course, is to try to keep the sexes in balance. It seems almost axiomatic that more men are interested in nudism than women.

The thinking goes that if single men are allowed, the balance will quickly tip heavily towards the male gender, making a less inviting environment for women.

However, many nudist resorts do allow single men. Check the resort's website first if you're not sure, or call or email the resort and ask.

Public nude beaches, however, typically don't have any limits on who can attend, so if that's where you're going, then as a single man you won't have any trouble.

What if I get an erection?

This is without a doubt the most common question that men have when they're new to nudism. The fear is understandable: we're so accustomed to nudity being sexualized, we assume we'll have a sexual response to the nude environment.

In fact, most men are surprised by how rarely this occurs. After they are nude for the first few moments, most men never think of it again.

Why is that? Our minds seem very much attuned to the context in which we're viewing nudity. In our conscious mind, we assume that more nudity will equal more sexuality. Yet our brains get completely different signals in a nudist venue. For whatever reason, we don't feel the same responses we would in a sexualized environment.

Now, about those first few minutes. Some men do feel a rush of excitement as they disrobe for the first time, as they break the clothing taboo. This sudden adrenaline rush often can spur an unexpected excitement reaction.

Men who have an involuntary erection—for whatever reason—can easily deal with it, however. First, you always have a towel close at hand in a nudist venue; it's very easy to leave it casually draped over your shoulder to obscure the erection. Or you can place the towel on a nearby chair or chaise, and sit or lie down. No matter how intense the erection, it will soon disappear.

Remember that an erection is not something grotesque or unnatural. If nudists aren't ashamed of their bodies, why should they hide a perfectly normal and natural part of men's anatomy, working as it's intended? There are two main reasons.

First, the erection automatically sexualizes the nudist space. The lack of overt sexuality is one of the most attractive aspects of social nudism. A flaunted erection re-establishes the nudity as part of our society's same old sexualized space.

Second, it can make women uncomfortable. Nudist women typically don't mind being seen, even if the characteristics that make them physically attractive in a conventional sense are on display. However, an man who is obviously erect sends the signal that they are not being appreciated in the same way as others in the nudist space; they are being sexualized by the man, who is openly displaying his lust for them. Even if he isn't consciously thinking lustful thoughts, displaying an erect penis certainly sends that message.

It is always good advice, then, for men to be as discreet as possible about their erections in a nudist space. And if you find that you are continuously or repeatedly erect in nudist venues, you might want to spend some time reflecting on why that might be before you next return.

Questions from Women

What if I'm on my period?

Women who are menstruating when they want to attend a nudist venue have several options. Many women choose to use tampons or a menstrual cup, which enables them to remain nude. Other women cannot or choose not to use tampons, and while they need to, they simply wear shorts or swimsuit bottoms.

Nudism is a preference for being unclothed, but even in a nudity required venue, it is understood that women may have specific needs. There is no shame for these necessities, so do whatever is necessary to feel comfortable. Nudists understand.

How do I keep creeps from harassing me?

There's no getting around it: women get harassed by men. Women may feel that being nude puts them in a position of great vulnerability.

This is one argument for approaching nudism through resorts or local organizations first, rather than nude beaches or unsanctioned nudist areas. Nudist clubs have a vested interest in excluding men who make women feel uncomfortable, and will be happy to take them aside and speak with them if it's a first complaint, or force them to leave the club if it's a pattern.

In general, nudists are aware of how women might feel in a mixed nude situation, and try very hard to make women feel comfortable and safe. Certainly, many nudist men make a point of being supportive and helpful to ensure that the women around them do not feel targeted or harassed. (If you are a man in a naturist setting, please do your part to make the experience a positive one for women.)

The freedom and comfort of nudism are meaningless without a sense of security and personal safety. If you feel threatened or uncomfortable, make it known to the club management. And if they do not rectify the situation, remove yourself and tell others. You should never accept a harassing environment, and all nudists should be aware of this and work to make the situation better.

Your First Outing

You've thought a lot about nudism now. You've probably spent some time nude in the comfort and safety of your own home. At some point, you're going to say, "There are places out there where people are just like me, and hang out nude together as though it's the most natural thing in the world. Shouldn't I go join them?"

You're ready for your first nudist outing.

You have a number of options if you're looking to try nudism for the first time. We'll discuss some of those below.

Where to Go

Your first time going "out" is, for many nudists, a really big event. If you've never done it before, but you're interested, you might have already done some research on the venues around you. If not, that's your first task.

Finding Local Nudist Opportunities

The first thing to do, of course, is an internet search. Search for "naturist places" and the name of your city or region. Make sure you have some specific places included in your search. As you can probably imagine, a number of pornography sites masquerading as nudist sites will inevitably appear in your search results. Using specific town names helps limit them.

If there are nudist resorts or official nudist beaches in your area, you'll probably find them among the top results in your search. You might also find some listings of nudist venues, whether in your region, your country, or worldwide. It's good to open a few of these links.

Unfortunately, the nudist community is not well organized, so there is no authoritative, central, complete, up-to-date database of legitimate nudist venues. As a result there's a certain amount of trial and error involved, and there is no single website that will give you all the answers at this point.

However, some websites are still better than others. One of the best ways to find a nudist venue is to check the website for your region's or country's nudist organization. Most of their websites have excellent lists of legitimate nudist venues. They might not list even well-known unofficial locations, but they're a great place to start.

Check **Appendix A** for a list of the web pages of some of the larger naturist organizations in the world.

Naturist Clubs and Resorts

One of the best ways to get comfortable with nudism for the first time is to go to an actual nudist club or resort. The entire concept of a nudist club is to make a comfortable, pleasant experience for people who enjoy being nude.

There are a number of advantages that clubs have over other nudist venues. First, they will tell you anything that you, as an inexperienced nudist, want to know. They are explicit about their rules—you can usually read about their rules, their code of conduct, their amenities, and everything else about them online. And if you have questions, you can ask the staff.

The first time I went to a nudist club, I was unsure whether I was supposed to be undressed before I registered or not. I decided to keep my clothes on until I had actually registered for the day. But at the desk, I asked what people typically did, and the staff member told me "Oh, you're fine to be nude anywhere on the club grounds, so it's up to you." That took the guesswork out of it completely. It was a small point of confusion, but it did cause me a little bit of uncertainty and self-doubt before I asked the staff about it.

Nudist clubs are also controlled environments. No one there is going to make you feel self-conscious for being a nudist. No one is going to judge you. No one is there for any reason different from yours: they want to hang out nude for a while.

What's more, most clubs are very careful about harassment on their grounds. If someone there is making you feel uncomfortable—leering, staring, making sexual comments, or making unwanted sexual advances—you can talk to the staff about it. Read the club's code of conduct if you want to know what to expect.

One thing that makes nudists particularly uncomfortable is gawkers, people—usually men—who don't want to be nude, but just want to ogle naked women. While they might come to nudist clubs from time to time, in general nudist clubs aren't where they congregate. And if they're acting creepy, the staff will ask them to leave.

The main drawback to nudist clubs is that they're expensive—some cost over $50 for a single day pass. This seems reasonable to many nudists, but it can be a significant expense for others. They also aren't common. I'm lucky enough to have two within an hour's drive of my home, but many people live several hours' drive or more away from their nearest club.

However, a nudist resort is still probably the best place to go for your first nudist experience. Research what's around you and see what your options are.

Non-landed Nudist Clubs

Many nudist clubs are located in rural areas to allow their members to enjoy an open, natural setting. However, nudists exist in cities as well, and often form official or unofficial clubs. Because they are an association and typically do not have a specific space where they congregate, they are referred to as non-landed nudist clubs.

One of the most common types of non-landed club is the nudist swimming club. In many cities in North America and Europe, these clubs rent out public swimming pools in the same way any group might, and have nudist swim nights. The shared cost isn't too high and they almost always want as many people attending as they can, so that they don't lose money on the pool rental.

These clubs can be more difficult to find. They often don't advertise heavily, because it might draw unwanted attention. In Calgary, for example, when a news article appeared about a nudist swim club, protests against the nude swim soon shut it down for fear that someone would publicly shame or even attack the nudists who attended.

So it might take a bit of digging. Nudist-themed online communities are a good place to start—go to your regional or national organization's website to see if they have a list. Another place to look is on sites that informal groups use to arrange meetings, like meetup.com. Often nudist groups will create events there, and if you add nudism to your interests, the site will soon be alerting you to nudist events happening near you.

Do take a look at the philosophy of the non-landed club before you attend an event, though. While most nudist swim clubs are legitimate, occasionally they are groups that use nudism as a cover to get together for sexual activities. (This might be perfectly legal between consenting adults—but it's not nudism!) It's usually not difficult to recognize the groups that are truly interested in nudism if you read a little bit about their purpose, history, and philosophy first.

One of the best things about local nudist clubs is that most of the participants are from the local area, unlike nudist resorts, which can attract people from anywhere in the world. So by attending a nude swim or nude bowling night, you are likely to meet nudists from your own community, which might be a plus.

Official Nudist Beaches

If you're lucky enough to live by a large lake or ocean, you might have an officially-sanctioned nudist beach near you. In Florida, New Jersey, Australia, Germany, Canada, and many other places, there are designated beaches where clothing is optional.

Beaches are often a new nudist's first destination for a clothes-free experience outdoors. There are few barriers to entry; typically you don't have to pay to go on the beach, and there are no barriers to single men, same-sex couples, and so on. You don't have to call ahead to find out if the beach is open. You just show up with your blanket and sunscreen, remove your clothes, and enjoy the sun.

One issue with official nude beaches, though, is that they are rare. It takes a lot of political will to designate a beach as clothing optional, especially in North America. Only a small proportion of the world's beaches allow people to take their clothes off without any fear of penalty or sanction.

Another issue is that most beaches are clothing optional—*not* nudist. Most people do stay nude or at least topless, but people are free to leave their clothing on, if they wish. This leads to gawkers who wander the beaches fully clothed for the sake of a voyeuristic glimpse of exposed skin.

It should be noted that many nudist resorts are in fact clothing-optional too, and may only require nudity in some parts of the club. But the barriers to entry and lack of enforcement in a public nudist beach means that a lot of people know about it, no one is prevented from being there, and gawkers are more or less free to gawk.

However, on many official beaches, there are so many nudists using the beaches that gawkers are less likely. It's amazing how, when most people are nude, having clothes on can feel weird and embarrassing! This effect leads to fewer voyeurs on the more popular clothing-optional beaches.

With their lack of barriers to entry, low cost, and anonymity, many people find clothing optional beaches a great option to start out as a nudist. If there's one near you, do some reading and see if it looks like a place you want to try.

Unofficial Nudist Spaces

There are only a handful of clothing-optional beaches in any given part of the world, but those aren't the only places people go nude together. Non-official nudist spaces are much more common. In fact, many officially designated clothing optional beaches started out as unofficial nudist haunts.

The most common unofficial nudist spots are beaches. In North America, for example, almost every major body of water has an unofficial nudist beach on it somewhere. And even with lakes and streams, there are waterfalls, creeks, and ponds that "everyone knows" is where you go to skinny-dip.

In fact, there wouldn't be much nudism in some places without unofficial nudist spaces. The state of California has no official nudist beaches, and yet people generally treat several beaches all down the coast as clothing optional. Even major nudist venues like Black's Beach near San Diego are not legally sanctioned, despite thousands of people using them.

However, there are more unofficial beaches than official ones. You're far more likely to find an unofficial space near you, and that can make a big difference. For many people, the unofficial nude beach might be a better option, or the only practical option.

The question is how to find these unofficial places. Some nudist organizations maintain lists of known unofficial places (my national organization, FCN, does this, while a major American association, AANR, does not). Some online nudist communities also have forums where users can contribute information on places to be nude.

It's worth reading as many reviews as you can before visiting an unofficial nudist beach. The first nude beach I ever visited would have been a much worse experience if I hadn't followed advice about bug repellent to keep the sandflies away, for example.

Read carefully about how to get to these places, too. These spots tend to become safe for nudism because they are out of the way, and non-nudists won't stumble on them by accident. One nudist-safe beach I know of requires you to walk down a very steep, narrow path down what is practically a vertical cliffside. And to get to Black's Beach you'll have a twenty-minute walk.

Something else to keep in mind with unofficial spaces: they don't have any amenities. You'll have to bring water and food if you're going to spend a while at an unofficial nude beach. And there are typically no lifeguards at these beaches, nor are they policed. That's not to say they're unsafe, but you'll need to decide whether they fit for you.

Your First Time Getting Nude

The very first time you participate in a nudist venue can be a nerve-racking experience. It's normal to feel extremely self-conscious or out of place. You're about to break a big societal taboo, and you might never have done anything of the kind before. It's natural to be nervous! Almost everyone you'll meet at a nudist resort has gone through the exact same thing at some point.

Wherever you've decided to be nude, the first to determine is when you're supposed to remove your clothes. If you're going to a clothing optional beach, you can remove them whenever you're ready, once you're past the point where nudity is sanctioned. At a resort, you can undress at your car, or after you've registered. If you're at a non-landed club swim, the locker room is almost always the right place.

The easiest way to determine whether you should undress is to look for other nude people. If others are naked around you, it's fine for you to be as well. Take your time, look around, and figure out where you'd like to get naked.

A piece of advice: get it over with quickly. It doesn't help to linger—take off your shoes and socks, walk a little further, take of your shirt, walk a bit more—this is a band-aid-off-quickly situation. When you've picked your point, stop. Take off your clothes just like you're about to change into a swimsuit or get in the shower. Put them away in your bag. Put on your flip-flops, locate your sunscreen, and you're there.

Another word of warning about this part of the process. If this is your first time ever being nude in a public or social situation, it's quite a rush. You're standing in nude opposition to all the things that were reinforced throughout your entire life. If you were ever mocked for not being fully clothed, or scolded for being too immodest; if your childhood classmates ever giggled at seeing a bit too much of someone's skin—all of that pressure could come bubbling to the surface at this precise moment.

It's more than that, too. I know that I felt a rush of sensation—every cell of my body seemed to come alive at once, feeling the sun, the air, the breeze. I've talked to many other nudists who felt the first thing on their first time, and often for several times after that as well.

That rush, that overwhelming feeling of physical sensation and mental and emotional freedom, is intense for many people. And for most of us, there's only one rush that is at all similar in our lives: a sexual thrill.

Getting naked in a nudist context the first few times is not, I stress, a sexual thing. But I have discussed it with numerous nudists, and the intensity, the sensations, the feelings of excitement mixed with fear... sexual thrill is the most common analogy for it.

Unfortunately, for male nudists, the similarity to sexual excitement can lead to an unwanted response—just at the time when you might be feeling at your most vulnerable! And this is why I bring it up: as a warning. It's not uncommon to become a little too excited, and get an erection (at least a little) your first time getting nude. Women do get a similar reaction too, but their response to it isn't as obvious as men's. For both men and women, though, it's a perfectly understandable and natural response.

And it's perfectly okay. It's a normal response for anyone brought up in a society that closely ties nudity and sexuality together. But it's worth being prepared. Make sure you have a towel ready when you start to get undressed. Drape it over your shoulder or hold it in your hand strategically.

You might find it much easier and less dramatic; you might find yourself almost overcome with anxiety and embarrassment.

It's fine. Take your time. Concentrate on the positive feelings, the great physical sensations that you're experiencing. Ignore any other people around you; trust me, they aren't paying any attention to you whatsoever. You're just yet another nude person in a place where there might be dozens, even hundreds of nude people. Wait it out. Breathe. Relax. Enjoy the feeling of being nude, of being one with your surroundings, of being your true, authentic self.

If you have to, take a walk. Not towards other nudists—off on your own, around the resort parking lot, or towards a less populated part of the beach. Enjoy all the new feelings you're experiencing: the way parts of your body move, the way your skin feels when it's completely uncovered, the way your private parts feel when they're exposed to the sun and the air.

Once you're ready to move on, guess what?

You did it.

Practical Tips

Going to a nudist venue is actually pretty straightforward: at least you already know what to wear! But it might be helpful for you to consider a few tips about visiting a nudist venue for the first time. Whether it's a clothing-optional resort, a nude beach, an intimate nudist board games night at someone's house, or a week at a secret all-nude tropical island, there are a few things you might not know before you arrive. Here are some tips to help with your first time being nude.

Nudist Etiquette

The simple rules of politeness among naturists aren't really that different from the etiquette for clothed folk. In fact, a good rule of thumb for nudist etiquette is, if you wouldn't do it while you had clothes on, don't do it nude! That said, here are a few rules of etiquette that you might find useful.

- **Don't stare**. This is a very common problem for new nudists. They have never been in a space like this, have never seen as much bare flesh as this in one place. It doesn't matter. Don't fixate on anyone's body. When you're talking to someone, look them in the eye—and nowhere else. A glance is fine, especially from a distance, but don't stare at anyone. Even if they don't notice, others will.

- **Don't comment on anyone's body.** Too often, new nudists think this is an acceptable subject of conversation. Their reasoning seems to be, since we're all comfortable with our naked bodies, shouldn't I be able to comment on other people's physical attributes? The answer is an emphatic *no*. Calling attention to others' bodies is extremely rude under any circumstances, and talking about people's bodies is absolutely wrong in an environment where everyone is supposed to be equal and accepted. This includes compliments; no woman wants to hear your thoughts on her figure, and no man wants to discuss his endowment. Leave your comments on people's bodies out of your conversation, full stop.

- **Keep sex out of it**. You might still make an association between sexuality and nudity; you've probably been told all your life that they're inextricably linked. But nudists typically go to some pains to keep the two ideas separate. By using sexually suggestive language or raising sexual topics in conversation, you're violating that approach. It's far safer not to talk about sex or sexuality at all in nudist conversation.

- **Be polite**. Sure, you're nervous—it's your first time at a nudist venue. Your nervousness might make you a bit more tense than usual. It's easy to forget the normal rules of social engagement and behave in a way that's out of character. Keep in mind that you're there to enjoy yourself, and don't get caught up on the small stuff. If you're frustrated or upset by something someone else says or does, take a breath and let it pass—you'll feel better for it.

- **Use a towel**. Nudists are pretty carefree, but for everyone's comfort and peace of mind, it's nice not to put your butt in a chair recently vacated by someone else's rear. Wherever you sit—no matter how briefly—put a towel under you. When you lie out on a chaise longue, cover it completely with a towel, with two if necessary. And that tendency for cleanliness extends to every part of your stay; shower before you get in the pool or hot tub, with soap and hot water. You don't want to be the one everyone notices for not protecting everyone else from your germs.

What to Bring

You'll want to be prepared when you arrive at a nudist destination. This is especially true with nude beaches and unofficial nudist spaces: there might be no services anywhere near where you're planning to spend the day. Here is a good checklist for preparing for your first nude day.

- **Towels**. You need at least one towel, maybe two. Oversized beach towels are perfect for your nude day. Nice, clean, fluffy towels are a great way to make your day more comfortable! Remember that if you're going to a nudist resort, towels are not just for drying off after getting out of the pool or hot tub. You'll sit on them everywhere—in the sauna, on deck chairs, or inside in the lounge. If you have room to pack more, it's always worth taking extra.

- **Sunscreen**. If you're going to be outside at all, you need sunscreen. Maybe you already have a good base tan—that's fine. Just make sure you have what you need to keep more sensitive skin, like nipples and genitals, from overexposure to the sun. And you'll need to cover parts of your body you might not be used to, like your buttocks and hips and breasts. Don't get caught up in the excitement of your nudist adventure; a bad sunburn is something to avoid, always.

- **Hat and sunglasses.** If you're outdoors, you might feel a little more exposed to the sun than usual. Having a hat to shade your face and sunglasses to cut down the glare might be a good way to feel more comfortable. Note that having sunglasses on doesn't mean you can stare at people. Yes, they will notice, and no, it's not okay.
- **Reading materials.** It's fine to spend your entire day tanning and watching the world go by. But you might also want to bring some reading materials—a book or a couple of magazines, for example, or an e-reading device. Remember that at some venues, electronic devices with cameras are absolutely forbidden in some or all of the venue's areas. Your phone or iPad might have to stay behind in a locker or your car. (As a writer I also bring a pen and notebook, but that's just me.)
- **A bag.** Whether it's a beach bag, a satchel, or a duffle bag, you'll need something to carry stuff around in. You've got your towels, bottles of water, snacks, wallet or

purse, money and credit cards, sunscreen, and hat. It's a lot easier if you have a bag to throw over your shoulder that will fit everything.

There—you're packed and ready to go. Off to your first nudist outing!

Nudist Organizations

Like almost every other hobby or lifestyle, there are groups to organize those who partake, and to improve the conditions for those who practice it. Nudists are no different: there are local, regional, national, and international nudist and naturist organizations.

What Do Nudist Organizations Do?

Nudists are often considered a "fringe" group in our society. There's little political capital to be gained by a government for passing nudist-friendly laws. It's up to nudists themselves to advocate for these changes themselves, and that is very difficult to do. A nudist organization, usually at the national level, is often the best way to pursue it.

A well-established organization with hundreds or thousands of dues-paying members has a great deal of clout with governments, compared to an individual. These members are all citizens and potential voters. Government workers and elected officials will usually be more interested in serving larger groups rather than individuals.

At the higher levels, nudist organizations usually work on the following issues:

- Lobbying for changes to civil or even criminal law to allow nudity in public
- Establishing clothing-optional beaches or areas
- Collecting information and making it available to members
- Monitoring and approving nudist resorts and clubs
- Cataloguing nudist and clothing-optional locations

- Advocating for nudists in the media and responding to media requests for opinions on nudism-related issues
- Providing well-researched, authoritative information about events to persons and groups involved in nudism

Groups that organize more locally work on many of these same issues as well. However, because they are more focused on a single area, they might work on other ways to improve the lives of nudists. They might have enough volunteers that they can organize, promote, and run events in secure, private, nudist-friendly venues, such as swims, bowling nights, and pub nights.

Nudist groups at all levels are powerful antidotes to society's erroneous and negative views about naturists. There have been examples in recent years where perfectly innocent nudist events were the focus of public outcry. In 2018 alone, nudist swims in Edmonton, Canada, and in North Yorkshire, UK attracted public outcry about children being naked at these events. Having multiple nudist groups with hundreds of members speak in defense of the event can change a disaster into a public relations coup.

In short, nudist groups are an important way to give nudism legitimacy, and to normalize the naturist point of view.

Why Join an Organization?

Whether or not you're a fully committed nudist, joining a formal nudist organization is a good idea. The benefits usually far outweigh the small membership fee.

The first objection that many people have to joining a nudist group is that they can get anything they need—information, community, and so on—for free online. This might be true for some organizations, but it definitely isn't true for nudist organizations. There are some legitimate online nudist organizations, but they are far outnumbered by illegitimate ones.

Why are so many groups illegitimate? It's the voyeuristic quality of the internet, unfortunately. When people discover that nudists are posting photos of themselves, the membership quickly explodes with people seeking nude photos.

There are some online organizations that do not require or even allow photos. These sometimes start up really well, but they present another problem: authenticity. There's no way to know that a profile represents an actual nudist, or is someone looking for female nudists to pester for photos, or someone satisfying other, more prurient interests.

It's far less common for people to join legitimate, established organizations if they aren't already a nudist. So if you want to be sure you're part of a group with actual nudists as members, and supporting real nudist values, join an organization that isn't just online.

Supporting these organizations is a small step towards big change. As groups gain members, their political clout and public reach increase. Societal change is slow and incremental, but you can help to speed things up by joining an organization. (You can help even more if you're able to contribute as a volunteer, too.)

One of the most important benefits to joining an organization is reliable information. You'll hear about issues involving nudism, issues that you might be able to help with (such as by signing a petition). You'll learn about new nudist groups and venues, or even established venues that you weren't aware of. And you'll get to know the people who are making nudism a reality around you. It might feel like a small thing, but so often we say "If only I had known." This is one way to make sure you'll know what's happening, when it happens.

Finally, becoming a member of an established organization helps to legitimize and normalize naturism, not only in general, but for you. By becoming a member you are making a commitment to nudism, and that can affect your own mindset. You'll feel part of a larger movement, and you'll know that others share your preference for nudism. It's another step towards accepting yourself as a nudist.

Your Nudist Life

Whether you have actually tried being nude with others or not, once you decide you are a nudist, you may want to make it a bigger part of your life.

You know, of course, that that doesn't mean you have to be nude all the time, or even under every possible circumstance. Naturism tends to be a component of people's lives, not an all-encompassing lifestyle. It's worth thinking about how it will fit into your day-to-day living.

The following sections explain some of the ways other people look at being nude as part of their overall lifestyle.

Types of Naturism

Nudism comes in many forms, and fits into people's lives in different ways. There are a number of terms used to describe different types of naturism that people practice. The following "types" of naturism are the most common ways people describe how they practice nudity.

No particular way is better or worse than the others. There is any wrong way to be a nudist (excluding problematic cases like exhibitionists). However, some people think, for example, those whose nudity is confined to their own home are not "real" nudists. Anyone who prefers being nude to being clothed is, in my view, a real nudist. But it's helpful to recognize that there are many different ways to be a nudist. Here are some of them.

Closet Nudist

There are many reasons people decline to share their nudism with others. For their own reasons, they may just not be ready to get naked anywhere but in private, and are finding their way into nudism at their own pace. These are closet nudists. They are typically nude only when they have their home to themselves, or in the privacy of their own room. Many nudists start out as closet nudists until they become more comfortable with being naked. It's important to avoid judging others for how they practice nudism. Whether or not we agree with their reasons for being only nude when alone, we have no reason to judge others or try to convince them to change their approach.

Solo Nudist

A solo nudist is typically someone who is only nude on their own. Some solo nudists are just not ready to be nude around other people yet (and if you're reading this book, you might be one of them). Some are in a situation where they're not ready to be open about being a nudist, perhaps because they live with family or roommates who are not comfortable with nudity, or their living situation is not private enough for nudism.

Home Nudist

Home nudists are nude some or all of the time in their home. Whether they live alone or with roommates, a partner, or their family, home nudists are comfortable being naked around the house. Those who define themselves as home nudists typically do not go to nudist venues like resorts or beaches.

Social Nudist

A social nudist may or may not be nude at home, but they do get nude outside of the home. Social nudists enjoy the way people interact when they are all nude, the different level of human interaction that nude people find with each other. Social nudists may visit nudist resorts, clothing-optional beaches, and other established nude venues. They might also be nude mainly in their own home or those of their friends, taking part in nude parties, nude board game nights, and other group activities. These nudists appreciate the social aspect of nudism, however they choose to get it.

Occasional Nudist

Some people enjoy being nude, and are willing to do so with others, but don't go out of their way to find nude opportunities. They'll take everything off to get into their friends' hot tub, and they'll go skinny-dipping along with everyone else when they're at the cottage, but they aren't nude very often otherwise. These are occasional nudists, also called recreational nudists. They tend to enjoy social nudity, but they don't necessarily share the philosophical outlook that drives many committed naturists.

Seasonal Nudist

Many nudists don't have the advantage of being naked outside year-round! Some who live in areas with long, cold winters only seek out nudist opportunities in the warmer part of the year, and choose these times to visit their local resorts or beaches. Seasonal nudists are in some ways the reverse of home nudists—they don't make nudism a part of their daily life.

Hard Core Nudist

Hard core nudists are nude by default. If they can be nude, they will be. They spend their free time in venues where nudity is acceptable, and they seek out places where they can be nude as much as they can. At home they are almost always nude. Many hard core nudists are also ambassadors for nudism, because they are so comfortable being nude they have no shame or embarrassment in enthusiastically telling others about why they love it so much. Some hard core nudists move to nudist resorts permanently, so that they can be without clothing for days at a time.

Ethical Naturism

Most nudists feel that there is more to nudism than taking your clothes off. An exotic dancer, an artist's model, someone taking a shower—these aren't nudists. Nudism is not just about taking your clothes off.

So what is it about? Ethical naturism is one interesting answer: the belief that nudity is part of a larger philosophy based on a lack of shame and embarrassment of a person's own image. Ethical naturists believe that to make someone ashamed or embarrassed about their body is immoral.

The purpose of naturism, following this philosophy, is to promote the wholeness of the human body, mind, and spirit. By shedding our physical encumbrances with others, we are better able to see and respect and ourselves and others.

Ethical naturists believe that society's negative attitude towards the human body's natural state results in a lack of self-esteem. In turn, they believe this reduces self-confidence and causes other emotional dysfunctions. They therefore work towards accepting of themselves, and of others, in their natural physical form.

This level of respect also leads ethical naturists to protect their physical environment as well. This is interpreted in a number of different ways. To some, it means protecting their own bodies, and being attentive to their own health, including both their physical and spiritual wellness. Many ethical naturists feel that they connect with nature more closely by removing physical barriers between themselves and the natural world, and so they choose to be more conscious of their role as a steward of nature.

Ethical naturism is therefore not something that one leaves at the door of the nudist club or at the edge of the clothing-optional beach. It doesn't even mean that one should be nude at every possible moment. It is instead a moral and ethical stance that informs how one sees the world. It is a set of values that a nudist can practice whether they are clothed or not.

Conclusion

Getting nude for the first time with other people is scary for some. It's stressful. It goes against values that many of us grew up with and see reflected in the world every day.

And yet, here we are, thinking about taking our clothes off.

Nudism can be a fulfilling pursuit that gives you fresh new energy—physically, psychologically, and spiritually. But it's still difficult to make that first bare-footed step into the world where clothes no longer matter.

With this book, you've learned about many positive aspects of the nudist life. You've also been armed with knowledge that will help you through those first tentative steps and—I hope— give you the ability to make nudism a meaningful part of your life, if that's what you decide you want.

Nudists represent every conceivable philosophical, political, and racial and ethnic part of the population. However, social, political, ethnic, and professional statuses are most often denoted with clothing. By being nude together, we remove these signals and start to recognize our sameness instead of our differences.

I hope you're ready to take the next step. If you are, then take your clothes off and join us!

Appendix A:
Nudist Organizations

International

International Naturist Federation
http://www.inf-fni.org/

North America

American Association for Nude Recreation
http://www.aanr.com/

Federation of Canadian Naturists
https://fcn.ca/

Fédération québécoise de naturisme
http://www.fqn.qc.ca/

The Naturist Society
http://www.naturist.com/

Europe

Association pour la Promotion du Naturisme En Liberté (France)
https://apnel.fr/

British Naturism
https://www.bn.org.uk/

Deutscher Verband für Freikörperkultur (Germany)
http://www.dfk.org/

Irish Naturist Association
http://www.irishnaturism.org/

Young British Naturists
https://www.bn.org.uk/ybn/

Other

Australian Naturist Federation
http://ausnatural.org.au/

New Zealand Naturist Federation
http://www.gonatural.co.nz/

South African National Naturist Association
http://www.sanna.org.za/

Appendix B:
Online Resources

Note: URLs and names of online resources change far more quickly than a book can keep up with. However, each of the resources listed below is well-established and has existed for a long time. I am hopeful that each of these resources will endure.

Communities

Reddit

reddit.com/r/nudism

Reddit is a huge site, but naturists have carved out their own corner of it. With news and discussion from nudists around the world, and with rules that strongly uphold naturist principles, this community has grown very well in recent years.

Naturist Community

naturistcommunity.com

Based in the UK, and largely used by UK users, Naturist Community is a reasonably active site that has shown some real staying power. The membership seems to largely be real nudists interested in socializing online.

NOOK

naktiv.net

Short for "Naked Online is OK", NOOK is a social networking site for nudists who want to engage in nude activities outdoors. Members can create profiles and post photos, but most of the activity is in the groups, user-defined forums and in users' news feeds.

Podcasts

Naturist Living Show

naturistlivingshow.com

The granddaddy of all the naturist podcasts out there, Stéphane has been publishing episodes regularly for over a decade. He's the owner of Bare Oaks and covers a breathtaking array of different topics in naturism. He's also a personal inspiration for me, and a great person to talk to about naturist topics.

The Naked Podcast

www.bbc.co.uk/programmes/p063wfw6

Two women, Jenny Eells and Kat Harbourne, do their regular podcast on BBC Radio Sheffield naked. They aren't nudists, but they recognize the difference that non-sexual nudity can make in how we relate to other people. Women's issues are given appropriate attention on their podcast but they have a lot of great guests and topics.

To the Nude Life

tothenudelife.com/podcast/

Martin is a full-time naturist (when he's not deployed overseas, of course) and is a true enthusiast for the nude life. He's also a chef and has had a lot of unique life experiences. His podcast is casual and comfortable, but based on a strong understanding of nudist ethics.

Blogs

Naked Wanderings

nakedwanderings.com

Nick and Lins left their home in Belgium in 2017 and haven't stopped since. They've travelled around the world to naturist resorts on every continent. Their very active blog provides honest and very personal reviews of everywhere they've stayed. They also share their thoughts on naturist philosophy and practice, and on their experiences in the nudist community.

Meandering Naturist

meanderingnaturist.com

Nude blogger Dan Carlson has been blogging about naturism for some years now. In addition to his reviews from his own naked travel, he provides well-considered opinions on nudism and how it is practiced today. He's been blogging since 2013 and shows no signs of stopping.

About the Author

Matthew McDermott is an author and consultant from Ontario, Canada. He has been actively participating in nude recreation for fifteen years.

He can be reached on Twitter at **@canudian1**, on reddit at **reddit.com/u/canudian1**, on his web page at **writenude.com**, and by email at **canudian1@gmail.com**.

Manufactured by Amazon.ca
Bolton, ON

38779790R00060